TARA M. KINGSLEY

GOD

CHANGE ME

Branded Gen, Inc.

2900 N Government Way #313

Coeur d'Alene, ID 83815

Brand People. Brand Products. Brand Industries.

www.brandedgen.com

FOREWORD

WHAT WOULD IT LOOK like if your soul were bared to the world? If you could be fully transparent, spilling out the ugly and the beautiful, the struggle and success, would you? Could you? Could you be that courageous? I'm not sure I could be, but my life has been immeasurably blessed by a woman who is.

Tara Kingsley, daughter of the One True King, survivor of the wilderness, and warrior in this world, has this courage. Her story of pain, sorrow, rebellion, and redemption outlines a rawness and honesty few have ever been able to express. The revelations that have changed her life and destiny in this world are a light on the hill, a beacon pointing the way to Jesus Christ. Her love and devotion to our Lord and Savior are inspiring and dictate how she lives her life daily— from her morning (and sometimes all day) time with

God to her battles with the Spirit and the humility with which she walks through her toughest moments.

Tara has taken the accumulation of her trials and blessings and has chosen not to swallow them into the depths but to organize them in her first literary work, in obedience to God. Tara was obedient in her call to write this book, as the chapters and content were literally given to her by God. In short, this book will bless you as it has blessed me. I pray you will read this with an open mind and open heart. See yourself in this story—your own struggles, your own obedience—and remember you are loved, you are worthy, and you are valued by the Lord of all creation, who looked down and found the world was left wanting without you in it. You may be in rebellion right now or you may have overcome rebellion. No matter where you are right now, remember this: You are still loved.

May the Lord bless you,

B. Toth

CONTENTS

INTRODUCTION

I DO NOT REMEMBER a time in my life when I did not believe in God, but I viewed God as simply my fairy godfather. I did not have a clear understanding of how much He genuinely loves me as I never saw myself as lovable. As a family, we went to church every Sunday, and sometimes we went to a midweek service too. Unfortunately, I really disliked church and do not remember a time when I ever wanted to be there. I did learn all the Bible stories though.

Which is why I knew the Bible story of Jonah. If I had to compare myself with one person in the Bible, I would say I most resemble Jonah. Jonah had a word from the Lord (Jonah 1:1–2), and instead of being obedient to the Lord, Jonah fled from God's presence. If you are not familiar with this story, Jonah's disobedience toward God found him in the belly of a very large fish. His actions also greatly affected several people whom he had dealings with along his path of disobedience. But there is another aspect of the story of Jonah as well. Another reason Jonah didn't want to do what God told him to do was because he didn't think the Ninevites deserved God's mercy and grace. For a very long time, I felt the same way about certain people in my life.

My story is not much different from Jonah's (minus the big fish) in that I started running from God's presence when I was about nine years old, mostly because I chose to believe the lies of the enemy rather than focusing on the truth in God's Word and how much He truly loves me. I believed I would die before I reached the age of twenty-one. I remember at sixteen, when I got my driver's license, it said under 21 until 1992. I thought, *Yeah right, like I will be alive by then.* I allowed the labels that this world put on me to shape my mind instead of believing the truth of God's purpose.

My first experience with marijuana was when I was nine years old. I blackmailed one of my older brothers, and he caved to my pressure. I was by no means an easy or obedient child. I was what looked to be a picture-perfect child at ten years old but then started using drugs as a young adolescent and ran away from home at the age of fourteen. I lied, stole from my friends, and had an extreme amount of pain and anger that I truly did not understand. I chose to use drugs and alcohol to numb the pain I was feeling.

I only finished three months of high school because I thought school was a waste of time and did not see it as important. I didn't think that I was going to live into adulthood, so what was the point? I allowed my emotions to rule my life and chose to only see the things right in front of my face. At one point in my life, at the age of fourteen, I was completely out of control and did not care if I lived or died. I remember wondering, *What is the point to my life?*

I allowed Satan to use things like comparison, self-loathing, and hatred to shape me as an adolescent. I saw everything in my life as someone else's fault, and my bad attitude was because of someone else's actions. I was never challenged, because I thought I was always right and the world owed me something.

God, Change Me

I believed my life sucked, and it was someone else's fault, not mine. I believed what the Bible said but didn't understand why my life was such a train wreck. It wasn't until much later in my life that I realized I really didn't know who God was at all. This book is the story of my life from walking in sin to rising up with Jesus in complete understanding and His glory.

CHAPTER 1

Complete Frustration

MY PARENTS HAVE BEEN married for over fifty years. I am one of three children, the only girl and the youngest by six and a half years. My mom was seventeen years old when she had my oldest brother, and my dad was nineteen. My parents were foster parents before I was born, but they stopped fostering after they adopted my middle brother. His biological mother drove through a sliding glass window while on drugs and could no longer care for him, so my parents adopted him. I was born in 1971, when my mother was twenty-four years old.

Some of the first memories I have of my childhood

are traumatic. I guess that makes sense because those types of memories tend to stick with us. My first memory as a child was when I was about two years old. I was at a swim party for my oldest brother's baseball team. I remember not understanding why I couldn't get into the pool. My mom kept telling me, "No, you can't swim." I, on the other hand, had no idea what swimming was. I just knew that all the kids were in the water, laughing and having so much fun. Her instructions made no sense to me. I thought she was keeping me from having fun, and that seemed so unfair. So when everyone was distracted with lunch, I walked right off into the pool and immediately sank straight to the bottom. I clearly remember standing on the bottom of the pool, looking up, and thinking, *Swimming doesn't seem so fun.* It was peaceful and quiet under the water but not the fun I had observed the other kids having. Suddenly, I saw a hand reach into the water, grab me by the top of my head, and pull me straight out of the pool. It was my oldest brother, who saved my life that day.

I can also recall the first dream I ever had. I woke

up remembering the scary events that I was certain took place in reality. I'm not sure who let me watch the movie *Jaws* when I was around five years old, but I had a dream my mom had been attacked by a shark. The shark had bit her leg, but the fluid seeping out of her leg was this yellow syrupy-looking stuff, not red blood. When I woke up, I bolted into her room, all freaked out. She was sitting on her bed putting lotion on her freshly shaved legs. I could not believe she wasn't hurt or maimed from the shark attack. I remember her explaining to me that it was just a dream. The yellow liquid instead of blood puzzled me for a long time.

My mom's dad, Grandpa John, died when I was five years old. He had cancer that started in his lungs and metastasized to his brain. This was the first time I remember seeing my mom cry. I didn't understand death, and none of this made sense to me. They had an open casket at the funeral, but the day before, they decided to have a private viewing for our family. I remember my dad holding me over the casket, and I did not understand why my grandpa didn't get up out of there. He looked alive to me, except his eyes were closed like he was sleeping. He looked healthy. I wanted to touch his face, to check to see if he was really gone. My parents let me place the back of my right index finger under his nose to see if he was breathing. To this day, I can still remember how his cold skin felt on my finger. I was well into my twenties before I could go to a funeral without breaking out into laughter because of how that earlier experience affected me.

As a child, I would wake up in the middle of the night from night terrors, unable to breathe. Every one of these experiences was terrifying because they would leave me gasping for air. My mom would take me into the bathroom and turn the hot water on in the shower, and the steam would help me breathe normally again. I'm not sure how long this happened before my mom took me to the doctor, and I was prescribed Tussionex, which is a Schedule II narcotic. This narcotic was supposed to help me. It was a yellow syrupy liquid, just like the stuff coming out of my mom's leg in the first dream I remembered. I truthfully do not know how often this medicine was given to me. However, I do remember being under ten years old, climbing up to the medicine cupboard, and drinking it straight out of the bottle. I knew this was wrong and hid this from my family.

From a very young age, I knew there was something different about me, although I could never put my finger on it. The devil started lying to me and would tell me things like, "Your family doesn't really care about you. Look at all those freckles! Your legs are skinny and way too long for your body. You are ugly." I believed these lies and do not remember anyone ever telling me anything different. I felt trapped in a family where I thought I didn't belong. This was another lie that I believed, and partnering with this lie is what led me to a cycle of painful living.

I didn't understand why, as a small child, I was drawn toward strange sexual behaviors. I played weird forms of doctor with my friends. I would ask them to let me see their private parts, examine them, and show them how good it felt when I touched them. I also would make up games that always ended in touching my friends' privates or them touching mine. I did not know what that meant or where these feelings and thoughts came from. I seriously thought I was the spawn of Satan because of my mind, my thoughts, and the actions I was drawn to. I pursued what I perceived as love and was very confused about why these actions made me feel dirty and ashamed.

When I was nine years old, my mom and dad left me home alone with my brother and his friend. That was the day I proceeded to blackmail my brother. I told him that if he didn't smoke pot with me, I was going to tell my mom that he was growing and smoking marijuana. He caved, and I smoked marijuana for the first time. We were right in the middle of smoking when my mom walked in and caught us in the act. I remember thinking, *I am so busted!* My mom took me into the bathroom and, pointing at my reflection in the mirror, said, "Look at how red your eyes are! Why would you do this?"

I responded with "I don't know…." I didn't get in trouble, and this was never discussed again, not even with my father. I didn't use marijuana again until seventh grade. However, I was still using the Tussionex.

I proceeded to grow up in a home where I was not disciplined for anything I did, and I did a lot! Every time I would do something wrong and my brothers were involved too, they would get in serious trouble, while I would always get away with no discipline. Maybe my parents thought my brothers were being a bad influence on me or they thought that I was too young to know what I was doing was wrong. However, I knew. I remember as a small girl when my brothers got in trouble and were spanked, it would make me so angry at my parents. I didn't think they loved me because I never got reprimanded or in trouble. I think I felt left out and sensed that I was not a part of this trouble that I deserved to be spanked for. I slowly began to hate them and despise their actions, or lack of actions, where I was concerned. This lack of discipline made me feel unimportant, unloved, and not included.

I didn't have a lot of friends, but the friends I had I treated horribly. I had two friends who lived down the street from me, and they would come over before school so we could walk together. Sometimes they would have to come to my room because I wouldn't be out of bed yet. I would literally throw things at them and yell at them to get out of my room. I was a spoiled little tyrant. I was angry and thought no one cared about me.

CHAPTER 2

It's Them, Not Me

I HAVE ALWAYS BEEN an incredibly gifted athlete. When I was five years old, my mother put me in gymnastics. I excelled very quickly and was helping my instructor, Veda, lead classes when I was about six or seven years old. She used me as the model, and I would show the younger students how to perform certain moves. I really fell in love with gymnastics and wanted to be at the gym more often than not. I will never forget the first time I did a standing back flip. That feeling is truly unforgettable. During the same time, I began playing soccer, which I was also very good at. There were no all-girl soccer teams back in the mid-70s, so I played on a boys' team. I loved soccer but not more than I loved gymnastics.

When I was ten years old, my parents put my brothers and me in a private ski club. I did not enjoy being in this ski club but was forced to go every weekend. My brothers and I went skiing every weekend at different ski resorts in Northern California and Nevada. My oldest brother used to tell me that the bus was going to leave me if I were late, so I would only ski for half the day. The second half of the day I would sit on the bus and wait because I seriously thought I would get left behind. This left plenty of time for me to grow in my hatred towards both my oldest brother and my parents.

My hatred of my family continued to grow as I progressed into adolescence. When I was around twelve years old, my gymnastics coach started talking to me about the Olympics. My coach made me feel like I had a chance to train and go to the Olympics, and his words and encouragement filled me with excitement! I remember after gymnastics class running to tell my mom what my coach had said. My mom's reply was

"We can't do that. I can't leave your brothers, your dad. We can't afford that." I didn't understand why this was her reply. I decided to quit gymnastics. What was the point of continuing to do something if it was clearly never going to lead anywhere? My resentment and anger toward my mom continued growing.

I still played soccer and was really good at not just the physical game but the mental part of the game as well. I went with a friend who was trying out for the San Juan Competitive Soccer League. I watched her try out and really wanted to try out too, but my mom said that it was only for rich people. Again, I felt like there was no point in all the work I had put into this sport I loved so much, so I quit soccer too.

I can remember crying and telling my mom that I didn't feel like they loved me at all. I truly did not believe they did. I compared what I saw in other households to what was happening in my own house and blamed my parents for everything. My friends were doing things like playing competitive soccer and going to summer camp. I felt like I did not get to do the things I loved to do but instead I had to do what my parents wanted me to do. I allowed my heart to grow cold and hard toward them and God. My mom didn't understand my feelings and told me, "You are our daughter. Of course we love you." This didn't make me feel any better, and I continued to believe that no one cared about me. This discussion left me feeling the same way I did when we first started talking—unloved, worthless, and useless— and I hated myself along with my family.

I made some poor choices as a pre-teen and teenager that shaped me into a manipulative and cunning person. I knew how to get what I wanted and was doing all kinds of things behind my parents' backs before the age of thirteen. My heart was way past broken by the time I was fourteen. I didn't care about anyone or anything by this time in my life. I didn't even care about myself. I even carved the initials of a boy I liked into my ankle with a needle. The pain felt good to me.

As I entered seventh grade, I was a decent student, but I immediately started hanging out with the wrong kids, mainly because my "friends" were sick of me and the way I treated them. I started smoking marijuana and sneaking out of the house at night to meet my new friends and boys. I never snuck out of my own house but would always stay the night with friends and sneak out of their houses. For some reason, I thought I would get in more trouble if I were caught at my house. I think it was because my dad was home at night, and I truly didn't know what he would do if he caught me doing something wrong. I knew my mom would do nothing.

I did finally sneak out of my house one night, and I was super nervous about sneaking back in. Rightfully so, because my dad was sitting in the dark in the front room. Just as I closed the door, he turned on the light and said, "I'm glad you're back and safe. Get in bed." No yelling, no discipline.

I gave my virginity away at the age of fourteen during the summer between eighth and ninth grade. He was seventeen, and it was the summer of 1985. He was nervous, whereas I literally didn't think it was a big deal. I remember him saying, "We don't have to do this." I responded with "Yeah, it's fine. It's no big deal." I had no self-worth, and all I wanted was to feel loved or something to make me feel better about myself and my life.

I was also fourteen when I decided that I could not take my family any longer. I felt like they didn't care if I was there or not, so I ran away from home about three months into my freshman year of high school. I lied and told my friends that my parents were gone and I didn't want to stay at home alone. Some of my friends' parents called my parents, and some didn't. I remember spending several nights on top of the snack bar at Phoenix Field in Fair Oaks, California. My mom told me that I could not come home unless I went to the Neighborhood Alternative Center in Sacramento and turned myself in as a runaway. After I completed their program, I was welcome home. I wrote this poem while I was searching for myself.

Sin and Glory

I am soft as I reach the end,
but every emotion inside leads to sin.
I want the best, but is that the issue?

It's Them, Not Me

No, I think not, I need to listen.
What is it I listen for?
It's a soft, sweet whisper inside heaven's door,
His voice is gentle, yet firm,
it makes me stop as I long and yearn.
Dear Jesus, I pray, please help me to walk in
the right way.
Although I think that I am seeking Him,
how easy it is to fall into sin.
Pray at all times, it is a must;
don't dwell on your sins or the enemy will destroy us.
You see me now, so don't turn back,
because every time I slip away,
it's just that much harder to get back on track.
Glorify Me and I will show you a better today
yet a beautiful tomorrow.

I was in and out of my parents' home over the next
several months. When I was fifteen, they tried for
the first time to set boundaries and establish rules
for me. I was completely disrespectful and out of
control by that time and would have nothing to do
with their authority. All I could think and feel was
that this was their fault, not mine; it was them, not

me. The hate in my heart toward my parents and family continued to grow.

I knew at fifteen I would not finish high school, and I never did. I saw myself as a waste of skin and a complete failure; I thought a lot about ending my life. However, there was something that kept me from actually going through with it. I didn't know at the time what it was. I hated myself and wondered why I was even here. I couldn't understand why my life was the way it was, so I did the only thing that felt good, and that was allowing guys to use me. I did not value myself, so I started sleeping with guys. I was so naïve that I thought this was what love was.

CHAPTER 3

Help Me, God—I'm Drowning

My heart was completely numb. I honestly didn't even feel like I had a heart anymore. I worked and partied from the time I was fifteen, sometimes working three jobs at a time. I liked to shop and I had a car, insurance, and credit cards to use. Truthfully, I do not even remember what my parents or brothers were doing during this time in my life.

I grew to be deeply disgusted by myself, so I continued doing drugs to numb the overwhelming pain. As I looked for love, I was allowing myself to be hurt over and over again. I was in this cycle of pain and heartache for such a long period of time that it became the only thing I knew how to do. I believe God allowed this to happen the way it did because I never sought a way to make it stop. I had grown comfortable with this pain and was accustomed to living in these feelings.

In the summer of 1986, I met Daniel, the man of my dreams, at Folsom Lake in Northern California. I lied and told him I was sixteen, and he told me he was eighteen. In reality, I was fifteen, and he was nineteen. He was not the type of guy I was used to being with—no drugs, no alcohol, and he didn't want to be involved with anyone who used those substances. I quit everything because I was in love, and I thought this was what was going to change my life forever.

I called my mom, and with a little explanation, she let me come home; after a little time passed, my parents let Daniel move into our home. Daniel was from Auburn, California, and worked in Roseville. He moved in because he told my mom it would cut his commute to work from 40 minutes to 15-20 minutes, and my mom thought this was a great idea. All I wanted was for someone to love me. I really thought he did.

I still at this point did not understand that I was not being protected by my parents. I thought, if they think this is okay, then it must be okay. However, I was fifteen years old and did not want to be having sex every day, sometimes multiple times a day. The relationship with Daniel lasted a little over a year, but he was cheating on me with his ex-girlfriend. When I went to my mom to tell her, she said, "I knew he had been cheating because I found lipstick on his collar. I didn't want to tell you, because I thought you would leave home again." I had never felt so betrayed in all my life.

I got a job with my best friend at Copeland Sports in the Sunrise Mall when I was sixteen. She worked in apparel, and I was a cashier. I immediately became involved with another employee, who was at least five years older than I was. We saw each other for about three or four months. He took me on a date wine tasting in Amador County one day, and soon after this date, I found out I was pregnant. I remember being afraid to say anything to anyone. I told him that I was pregnant, and he told me, "If you don't have an abortion, I will never talk to you again."

When I told my mom, she said, "No matter what you choose to do, I will stand by you and help you, even if you have an abortion. After all, it is just a mass of cells at this point."

I remember telling my best friend what he said; she stayed friends with him, and I had an abortion. I never heard from him again. My heart had never ached like that before, and it has never ached like that again since I made that choice.

The lasting emotional impact that abortion leaves behind is not worth it. I felt fragmented, like tiny pieces of myself were being peeled off like flower petals. I knew I was messed up from that choice, but I had no idea the consequences or the impact that one action would have on my life. My heart felt wounded beyond repair.

Over the course of the next four years, I worked, partied, and used every drug that was available.

I wanted to numb myself from the pain of all the betrayal I had experienced. I was in the world, and the world was in me. I grew in hatred toward my parents but worked and partied so hard that I really didn't see them much. Truthfully, I just wanted to get out of their home. Working and partying until 2 a.m. accomplished that. I left out the fact that I had a fake ID....

I started partying in bars when I was about eighteen years old. I had an older brother, and because of his friends, I got into all the bars in my hometown. I used to always say, "What do they expect us to do, sit around and watch TV?" I was not a stay-at-home type of kid. I needed something constructive to do, and I couldn't find anything. I looked to the previous generation, and they were all partying too. This led me down a road that created all kinds of deficiencies in my growth into adulthood.

I realized when I was twenty years old that I could not just stop smoking marijuana. At the time, I wasn't too concerned because I didn't see it affecting anyone except me. I was completely clueless about the spiritual aspect of allowing Satan to control that part of my life. I seriously thought I could continue in that lifestyle because I didn't do it in front of my family. Why would it hurt anyone other than me? I was the only one being affected by my actions. This was one of many lies I believed.

I met my son Dylan's father through some friends I had previously worked with. He was nice and kind, and he treated me amazingly. I used him, didn't respect him, and then got pregnant at nineteen years old. I didn't know I was pregnant until I was well into my second trimester. Abortion was not an option by that point, thank God. At first, I wanted to get married, but I soon realized that getting married was exactly what my mom and dad had done, and they were the last people I wanted to be like. I told him that I did not want to marry him, because I did not love him. He threatened me and said he would take my son away as soon as he was born. I lied and told him that the baby wasn't his. He changed his phone number, and I never heard from him again.

This is why I had to rely even more heavily on

my parents for support. My mom was a huge part of Dylan's life. She would watch him for me whenever I wanted. I continued to party and use drugs for the better part of his life. I tried to contact his dad about three months after he was born, but he didn't reply. When Dylan was between four and five years old, he did meet his dad, and when we went over to his house, Dylan got to meet his paternal grandma. Dylan saw them a couple of times, but his dad never reached out again. I truly believe this was the biggest loss for him. Dylan is the greatest son a mom could ever be blessed with.

I worked for a large commercial real estate firm in the early '90s but was only there for about six months or so. There were about twenty men and one woman I worked for, answering the phones and keeping their files in order. I met a man named Devin who worked there at the firm. I asked different friends who worked there about him and found out that he would not date anyone whom he worked with, so I quit that job right after Christmas 1992. I went back to beauty college to finish and obtain my license as a cosmetologist while working as a cocktail waitress at a bar and grill. I graduated from beauty college and began my career as a cosmetologist in 1994.

It was Super Bowl time in 1993, and I decided to call Devin. I asked him what he was doing for the Super Bowl. While we were talking, he ended up inviting me to go to a Super Bowl party with him. We had sex on our first date—I'd never done that before.

Devin had been married before and had a son named Jack. His ex-wife was crazy. I remember the first time I stayed the night at his house. She showed up in the middle of the night and literally started throwing rocks at the windows and screaming that she was going to kill Devin, Jack, and then me. For some reason, I didn't see this as a red flag.

Our relationship was so bizarre. I worked full-time doing hair making roughly $50k a year. I took care of Devin's home, drove Jack to school every day, and made dinner every night. Devin made $500k a year and would not pay for one single thing that had to do with me or Dylan. One year Devin won a fully paid trip to Hawaii for four. The only way that Dylan could come on the trip was if I paid for him, so I did.

I remember thinking that if we got married, it would change everything for the better. We were together for six years before we got married. My parents paid for the entire wedding except the photographer. This marriage ended eighteen months later because of domestic violence. I caught Devin in a lie, and he punched me so hard in my arm I could not straighten my arm for five weeks. I lost a large portion of my clientele because I could not work. My divorce was finalized in October 2000.

CHAPTER 4

God, Rescue Me

IN SEPTEMBER 2000 I was in Tahoe with a girlfriend, Susie. We were staying at my timeshare at the Ridge in South Lake Tahoe. She asked me if her friends, Bryan and Tom, could come up and stay because Bryan was an avid snow skier and wanted to ski the next day and Tom was a gambler. I knew Tom and had smoked marijuana with him and Susie before. I told her that was fine. We were planning on partying that night at the casinos, and I figured the more, the merrier.

I took ecstasy that night for the first time. That night was completely out of control. I could not believe how good that drug made me feel. We danced and gambled until the early hours of the morning. I completely forgot about the fact that I was about to be divorced for the first time. We partied all night and went to sleep when the sun came up. The next night, another one of their friends, Travis, came up and brought more ecstasy. We partied for another night. Bryan wanted to have sex with me, but I said no because I was still married. Bryan knew all the right things to say and do, but I still said no.

I started dating Bryan when my divorce from Devin became final. We bought our first home together in Shingle Springs, California, in September 2001. This was by far the most volatile relationship I have ever survived. We drank together, we used drugs together, and I got pregnant. I was distraught and cried out to God, "What am I going to do?"

When God answered, He said, "If you have this baby, it will be the hardest thing you have ever done in your life." I thought, *Ha! Bring it on!* I felt like marrying him would change things, but it didn't. We got married on September 27, 2003, when I was nine months pregnant. Our daughter, Aspen, was born three weeks later. As soon as we got married, he treated me like his property. Instead of a marriage certificate, it was like he obtained ownership papers of our daughter, my son, and me. He treated us awful, and I have never been so terrified in all of my life.

When Aspen was eight months old, Bryan got super angry at me and threw the TV remote at me while I was holding her. I still believe to this day that God protected her little head from getting hit by that remote. My marriage was so terrifying that I never knew what violent thing would happen on any given day. I needed help and wanted to leave Bryan, but I was scared.

Our entire marriage was terrifying for me as Bryan would cuss and scream at me most days. One night I came home from work late because I went out for a drink with a coworker. Bryan was asleep on the couch, and he, along with the entire downstairs, smelled like alcohol. Aspen was upstairs, asleep in her room. I woke Bryan up and started to talk to him from a chair that was close to the doorway to the kitchen. Bryan became enraged, stood up, grabbed me by the arm, and swung me around, throwing me from the front room into the kitchen. He apologized, and we had sex because I was terrified and didn't know what he would do next. I thought doing that would make things better. He left the house afterward.

He came home at some point in the early morning. When I woke up that morning and went downstairs, he was passed out on the couch, and the entire first floor of our house smelled like alcohol. I called the police because I was scared of what was going to happen when he woke up. When the police got there, I told them what had happened the night before. I had two visible bruises, one shaped like a handprint on my right arm and one on my neck from where his thumb hit me as he threw me from one room to the other. I didn't even see the bruises myself; the sheriff pointed them out to me. We separated in August 2005, and I obtained an emergency three-year restraining order against him.

Our home needed to be sold along with all the animals we had acquired over the four years we were together. We had goats, chickens, geese, and two horses. I am serious when I say selling the horses was the most painful loss of my marriage. Because of the restraining order against Bryan, it became my responsibility to do this on my own. I was having a hard time holding everything together in my life and was still struggling with marijuana. My stress level was at an all-time high.

One day while I was changing Aspen's diaper, all of the sudden Aspen said, "Mom, you are forgiven." She was only eight months old and definitely not speaking in full sentences.

In shock, I replied, "What?"

Again, she said, "Mommy, you are forgiven." I fell to my knees while holding her on the changing table and cried my heart out. I knew that was God speaking to me through my daughter. Jesus gave me the strength and confidence after that experience to leave that volatile marriage.

I finally found the courage to get the help I needed. There was a place in Placerville called "The Women's Center." I called there and was able to talk to a counselor immediately. I told her everything that was going on and made an appointment to go to an in-person intake session. During this session, they helped me take all the steps I needed to protect myself and my children.

I spent the next ten months attending domestic violence counseling. I learned why I allowed this pattern to be in my life and that I was not the only person in the world to allow this type of behavior in my life and around my children. I learned that I was worthy, I was forgiven, and my life mattered to my children. I learned, in fact, that I did have choices. I could control my actions and was responsible for my actions only. This is such a basic thing, but I did not understand this previously because my bad choices always changed things. I spent a lot of my life being angry at what I thought was everyone else's fault. It soon became crystal clear to me that I needed to change the choices I was making, but I did not know how to do it.

CHAPTER 5

Revelation—I Can Only Change Me

AFTER THE DIVORCE, WHILE sitting in a domestic violence group, I had an epiphany. I was in control!

The chairs would be in a horseshoe shape, and the leader would sit at the opening, facing us. Every week the women to the right of the leader were veterans of the group, and the women to the left were typically the newbies. We would go through several minutes of positive affirmations and meditation at the beginning of the group time. Then we would move into the sharing portion. The veterans would always share and talk about their own personal experiences. Every time a veteran would talk, I would think to myself, *Oh wow, I have been there. I've experienced that.* This made me feel like I wasn't alone. I seriously thought I was the only person on the planet who was dumb enough to stay in a relationship where I was being abused.

Each week I would go back to this group, and each week or two a veteran would have graduated and a newbie would be there. I remember thinking to myself, *I can't wait until I am sitting in that last chair before graduation.* It took me ten months of going to this group once a week for two hours before I finally made it to that final chair. It was through this experience that I learned I was not alone, I had control over my life's choices, and I could make better choices. I realized that I could control my actions and was responsible for my actions only. I felt like this was such a basic thing to understand. However, I did not understand this, because my choices (using drugs and alcohol) had always changed things in a bad way—until now.

I literally felt like I was walking through a fire

while I was going through my second divorce, but I began to see God show up in my life in some of the most profound ways. He was incredible. One miraculous way I saw God show up was during custody mediation. I was in the middle of court proceedings to determine who would have custody of our daughter, Aspen. I was asking for one hundred percent sole physical and legal custody because of Bryan's anger issues. It was during this period of time that I stopped smoking marijuana because I did not want to lose this court battle, and I knew that could happen if I didn't quit.

This was also a miraculous intervention by God as I had tried several times before and could not do it. When we went into the mediation, I was calm and collected, and Bryan flipped his lid over nothing and showed his true colors. The mediator and the advocate I had there for moral support were terrified because of the level of anger he exhibited. Needless to say, I was awarded sole physical and legal custody of our daughter. This was truly by God's grace.

Every time after this, whenever we went to court,

which was at least sixty times, Bryan was always represented by the council, and I always represented myself. There was only one time that I lost, and that was when I tried to get a permanent restraining order against him for physically assaulting our daughter. Other than that, I won every single time. This was truly God and His mercy showing up with His favor in our lives.

I realized when Aspen was very young that I did not want to be the reason that she didn't see her dad, and I made sure to not badmouth him in front of her. There was something in me that knew she would figure this out on her own, and sure enough, when she was about ten years old, she made the choice to not have a relationship with him. I am so grateful that God protected her and worked through me to teach her that she, too, could make choices that were best for her and her life. She has never regretted this decision. However, she does wish that her dad were different and that she could have had a relationship with him.

I was attending all the court hearings to determine

our divorce decree, and Bryan did not show up to one hearing. I felt pressure that I would have to figure out where Aspen, Dylan, and I were going to move or live. I remember hearing God tell me to wait, rent a place, and things would work out. I didn't listen to Him, because I allowed my stress and the devil to convince me that I needed to have a home for my kids.

After the divorce, I used my half of the money from the sale of our house to purchase another home. Dylan, Aspen, and I moved to Diamond Springs, California, in 2005. I asked my dad to put the house in his name because California law said if I purchased a house before the divorce was final, half of it would belong to Bryan. My dad purchased my home in his name and added my name after the divorce was final in January 2006.

At that time, Aspen was spending time with her dad once a week through supervised visits. I wanted to find something stable for her, so I thought church would be a good idea. I found the perfect church home for Dylan, Aspen, and me. After several months, I got involved with the women's group there and met with them weekly on Wednesday mornings. I was still searching to find someone that would help me to deal with my feelings and drug issues; I knew I needed to change.

I was incredibly ignorant and thought people at church weren't as broken as the rest of the world. One of the women, Sharon, from the Bible study I attended kept offering me pills like Norcos and Flexeril. Thank God I wasn't much of a pill taker. I confided in a leader at this church because I didn't know how to tell Sharon to stop. The leader told me she would not talk to Sharon about what I had told her, but she broke my trust. She went directly to her, and I immediately began receiving threatening phone calls from Sharon. I stopped going to church altogether. I also realized people are people, and just because someone goes to church, it does not mean they are any different from someone who does not. When I put my trust in people instead of God, it caused me to fall back into some of my old habits.

And even though old habits had surfaced, I heard the Lord say to me, "If you keep living your life the way you are living, you will lose everything, even Aspen." I didn't ask any questions because I knew exactly what He was talking about. I believed Him; I knew I needed to change. There was something deep within me that had been there my whole life that said I was created for more than this life that I had chosen. However, I didn't know how to make the changes that needed to be made. I tried in my own strength to make the changes I needed to, but I couldn't do it for more than a few weeks. I always came back to what was familiar, and for some reason, I found comfort in those wrong choices. I thought I would never be able to make the changes that I knew in my heart would save my life and my relationship with my children.

In 2007 my dad needed money for a personal reason and asked if he could refinance my house. He would pay the difference in the payment, so of course I said yes. There were only a few stipulations I had for him. First, don't pay $5k to refinance; second, do not get into a negative amortization loan; and lastly, do not take more than $50k because that would put me upside down in the house, where I would owe more than the house was worth.

I knew a guy and referred my dad to him. He was a friend of a friend from church. My dad refinanced my house. When I received the loan documents, I learned he paid $5k to do the refinance, he took a negative amortization loan, and he pulled out $48k for his personal problem. The bank would not work with me to get out of the negative amortization loan, therefore I was paying $2k per month for my house payment; $200 was going toward interest only and $1800 was being added back onto the principal that I owed. I stopped paying my house payment. I was angry and very disappointed, but my dad just said, "I didn't read the loan documents because I thought you knew the guy who wrote the loan."

I lost everything I had in April of 2009: my home, my car, and my business. I was completely distraught and didn't know how I would ever come back from this tragedy. Dylan was due to start his senior year of high school, but he decided to take his GED instead because I didn't have the ability to drive him to school for his entire senior year. I really beat myself up about this and felt like such a failure as a parent. As Dylan was now out of high school, he decided to go on a road trip. He headed up north on the coast of California with two of his closest friends. Their plan was to explore the north coast of California and Oregon and then they would rent their own house in Sacramento when they came back from the road trip.

Moving home to my parents was not an option; I could not imagine being back under their roof. I would have rather been homeless. I ended up moving to Mount Shasta City with a man named Erik, who was more than just a friend. He was involved in the cannabis industry, and that made it easy for me to go into complete escape mode for five months.

I didn't have any self-control when I was living in Mount Shasta. I would wake up in the morning and think, *Today I am not going to smoke marijuana.* About an hour later, I would be struggling. I tried everything to not do the thing I didn't want to do, but I failed miserably and daily by about 10 a.m. I was the heaviest I had ever been in my life, so I thought it would be a good idea to start walking for exercise. I was living in a house at the base of Black Butte Mountain, and it was absolutely beautiful there. There was the most amazing scenery outside, so I decided I would walk every day because it got me away from my struggle. I would walk about two or three miles, but without fail, as soon as I got back to the house, the struggle was there, and I would cave. This behavior went on for about two months.

One day I was bored and needed something to do, so I started looking around the house to see what I could find. There were a ton of books and cool old stuff sitting on the shelves. It wasn't my stuff, so it was like treasure hunting to me. I decided to look on the high shelf in the closet where I had remembered seeing some other books. I was curious to see what they were. I believe I was hoping to find something that I could read to take my mind off the struggle that ensued daily.

I reached up there and pulled down a book. It was a really old Bible. I opened it and saw it had belonged to Erik's dad. Charlie, Erik's dad, had passed away, but Erik had kept his Bible. I couldn't help myself, and I proceeded to flip through all the pages. There were a lot of notes, and it looked like it had been thoroughly read for a good amount of time.

Something grabbed onto my heart, and I was overwhelmed and started to cry. I didn't understand why I was crying or what exactly I was feeling, but I cried out to God and said, "What do you want me to do?" It was like there was another person in the room, and I heard Him say, "Go home!"

I was in shock, but I knew what I had heard! I told Aspen we were going to Nana and Papa's. I proceeded to grab all my stuff and threw it in the car. While I was driving toward Sacramento, I called my mom and asked her if Aspen and I could move back home. She said, "Yes, of course."

Over the next several months, I committed to spending daily time with God, really seeking Him as I sought to understand His character. He showed up every day and spent time with me. When I needed His presence, He came through for me like never before. Jesus brought me a sense of peace I had never felt before. I literally had nothing, but Jesus made me feel like I was important in everything!

CHAPTER 6

Why Aren't They Changing?

My children were seventeen and five years old when I moved back in with my parents. Dylan turned eighteen soon after we moved back to Sacramento and took off on a road trip with some of his close friends for his eighteenth birthday. I was nervous and didn't want him to go, but at the same time, I didn't want him to feel like I was trying to control him. He traveled up through northern California and had an amazing time with his friends. He ended up coming back to Sacramento and enrolling at American River College to obtain his horticulture certificate. He moved in with a few friends and began attending college.

When I first moved back in with my parents, the last thing I wanted was for them to interfere with my relationship with my children. I was very adamant about not enabling them, especially Dylan, and I asked my parents to not give him any money without him working for it. I didn't want to encourage any negative behaviors, and I didn't want him to be enabled and become unmotivated. I will not get into the details of this constant problem, but my request was not respected.

Dylan and I had a really close relationship in that he would not lie to me if I asked him a question, so I knew that my parents were enabling him. This brought back a plethora of negative feelings from my childhood, and all of the past feelings of anger and hatred toward my parents started to resurface. Along with those feelings of anger and resentment came the old habits of numbing them. I began to drink occasionally and smoke marijuana daily. I did not know how to deal with these feelings; they were too much for me to handle.

I had such a selfish attitude toward everything and could not believe I had ended up back in the place I swore I never wanted to be. I was angry and did not understand that this was all part of a bigger plan. I thought lashing out and telling friends about how awful things were would make things better. It didn't and just made me feel worse because I was so focused on the very thing that was keeping me in bondage. I was focused on the bitterness and anger and was allowing those things to hold me hostage. I did not understand where the anger was coming from.

Aspen was seeing her dad at this point in her life, so I had some free time each week. I was still making the choice to drink occasionally and smoke marijuana daily. I didn't realize at this point that the feelings of anger, bitterness, and resentment were growing toward my parents, and I felt like the only way I could survive was to stay numb. That is just what I did.

I decided that I needed to go back to school to do something other than cosmetology. I knew I would not be able to be a hairstylist forever, and I needed to take advantage of the opportunity my parents were giving me to live at home. I enrolled in my first class in the summer of 2010. I took a cardio circuit training class over that summer because I knew it would be hard to get the classes I needed in the fall, and this would give me priority registration for the Fall 2010 semester. I decided I wanted to do the prerequisite classes to get into radiological school and become a nuclear medicine technician. This was not something I prayed about, because I had started using drugs to numb my pain instead of letting Jesus heal me. I chose this path because it had the potential to get me out of my parents' home within three years in a field where I could earn over $90k annually. I figured I could provide a great life for Aspen with that income.

The first four semesters of junior college were me basically making up for the high school I never attended. This college thing was hard! I was so frustrated with my home life that I continued smoking marijuana daily. This didn't make school any easier for me. I felt so overwhelmed with all of the frustrations at home, and I truthfully didn't think I could take it. So I decided to do what I always thought helped me in the past.

In May 2011 one of my good friends, Jason, found out his wife was having an affair with his best friend. He fell apart and could not take care of his two daughters and his home all by himself, so I stepped in and started to help him. We lived about four blocks from each other. I thought this was perfect as it was one more thing that would take me away from my parents' home during the day so I wouldn't have to deal with the frustrations of my life there. Also, Jason's youngest daughter was Aspen's best friend from birth, so I was familiar with the girls, and they knew me; this made things easier on them too.

Jason had to have back surgery, so he was home and unable to work for about eight weeks. He poured his heart out to me about how he was hurt and broken and how this whole thing was a total shock to him. He had no idea the affair was happening, and it had been going on for seven years!

I felt so bad for him and his broken heart. While

Jason was sharing his feelings, his dreams, and what he thought his marriage was, something started happening in me. We decided that it would be easier if Aspen and I moved into his house, and Jason and I began a relationship that was more than just friends a few weeks after we moved in. I wanted to get married, but he wasn't ready. He was totally honest with me about his feelings. I stayed there because I really didn't want to go back to my parents' house, and I thought his feelings would eventually change. I never thought it would be me and my feelings that were going to change.

It is amazing to me how quickly time flies. Even though I was smoking marijuana daily and living at Jason's house, I knew I needed to make changes and decided that I would start reading my Bible daily again. I had heard a saying before that stated, "The Bible keeps you from sin, but sin keeps you from the Bible." I just couldn't kick the feeling that my life was full of sin. I prayed and asked God, "Is he the one for me?"

God answered and said, "If you stay in this relationship, you will die." It took me several months, but eventually I moved back into my parents' house. However, leaving this relationship proved to be much harder than I anticipated. I had feelings for Jason that didn't just go away. We didn't live together any longer, but I couldn't just walk away from him and the relationship we had established. As the months went by, it was like I was in a fog, just floating through each day.

I had spent several months after I moved back home trying to ignore my feelings for Jason by numbing them, using marijuana, and drinking on occasion. I did not know how to deal with my emotions any other way. I am still blown away every time I think of how hard I made my life by making the choice to believe the lie that this was the only way. I struggled with math in college mainly because I couldn't stop using marijuana. I made the choice to change my major from science to psychology as this eliminated all the math classes I would have to complete.

It was the beginning of November 2016, and God

challenged my heart again. He whispered to me as I was staring at Aspen, "You won't be here for her high school graduation if you don't make different choices." I began to weep, and I knew I needed to change. I desperately wanted to change, but I didn't have the strength to stop smoking marijuana every day. I was a complete mess. I think I was hoping that somehow I would just wake up changed one day. I wanted this change to come easily, but it was anything but easy.

Toward the end of November 2016, I received an invitation to Aspen's best friend's bat mitzvah. I was truly blown away and honored to even be invited. There weren't any other friends' parents invited, and Abbey said she considered me like her second mom. This made my heart feel happy. I sent back the RSVP that I would attend and would not be bringing a date. At this point, I was starting to feel something brewing in my soul.

CHAPTER 7

Father, Change My Heart

CAUGHT IN A VICIOUS circle, I needed to get out of my parents' house. Something would happen that would make me angry, and instead of dealing with my anger, I would numb it with marijuana and ignore the problem. I had been doing this for over twenty years and still knew no other way to handle things. I felt a serious push, like childbirth, and I wanted out of this house.

I decided to go to a family friend, Toni, who was an empty nester and asked her if Aspen and I could stay with them until I finished my bachelor's program. She began to tell me about some hard things she was going through and how she couldn't help me. She did give me some amazing advice though.

She said, "God can change your heart if you let Him."

"ME? Why do I need to change?"

She continued by saying, "If God doesn't change your circumstances, maybe He wants to change you."

Something happened inside of me, and I cried like I haven't before as I drove back to my parents' house.

I managed to make it through the holidays but literally dreaded every part of this season. Over the past several years, this time of year was the hardest because I listened to all of Aspen's friends talk about all the great gifts they got for Christmas. Money was extremely tight, and I was not able to give my kids the things I wanted to give them. At this point, I was counting down the years until I graduated and things would change.

After New Year's 2017, I felt this undeniable desire to change. I began to pray and ask God to change my heart toward my parents. I prayed, "Create a clean heart in me, O God, and renew a right spirit within me" (Psalm 51:10). I prayed this every day for two weeks straight, asking God to change me and my heart if He wouldn't change my parents. I didn't care if it literally killed me. The pain of staying the same became greater than the pain of changing. The time to change was now!

On January 15, 2017, I made the choice to stop drinking alcohol and to stop smoking marijuana. I knew this was the right choice, and I knew God would help me if I was obedient to Him. I told Jason that I wouldn't be coming over to his house anymore and that I needed to take a break for an unknown length of time. I told him I wanted to be obedient to God, and I knew this was the best choice for Aspen and me.

From that moment on, I had no desire to drink or smoke. I clung to God and His Word. I began to make different choices and filled my free time with serving at my church. Several months passed, and I was feeling stronger than ever. Cinco de Mayo came around, and an old friend called and asked me if I wanted to meet for a margarita at a Mexican restaurant just up the road from my house. What could be wrong with that? Before I knew it, I was two margaritas deep and feeling great. I had posted a picture and "checked in" on social media. I'm sure we are all familiar with the term "falling off the wagon." Well, I took a head dive directly off that wagon. I'm not sure if I called Jason or he saw my post, but he showed up at the restaurant, and I ended up leaving with him. I did all the things I had been so careful not to do during the last several months.

When I woke up the next morning, I felt terrible. Not hungover terrible but with feelings that I had let God down terribly. All of a sudden, God spoke to my spirit and reminded me about Matthew 12:43–45, "The Unclean Spirit's Return": "When the unclean spirit is gone out of a man, he walketh through dry places, seeking rest, and findeth none. Then he saith, I will return into my house from whence I came out; and when he is come, he findeth *it* empty, swept, and garnished. Then goeth he, and taketh with himself seven other spirits more wicked than himself, and they enter in and dwell there: and the last *state* of that man is worse than the first. Even so shall it be also unto this wicked generation." I wish I could say that I immediately got down on my knees and asked God to forgive me, but I didn't.

The next eight weeks were horrible. Jason had got involved with another woman he had met on a dating app, and I didn't realize this until sometime later. My heart was torn; I thought I had made a mistake, and I wanted him back. He wanted to be in a relationship with both of us but didn't want to tell her. That was when I cried out to God, and once again, He rescued me. On July 12, 2017, I cut all ties with Jason. God was so merciful and gave me His grace. This was still a very hard process for me to go through, but once again, God took all ungodly desires away from me.

I enrolled in my last semester at American River College in the summer of 2017. I had one last sociology class to complete to earn an AA in sociology. I had been accepted into California State University of Sacramento and was planning to start their sociology bachelor's program as a junior plus in the fall of 2017. It was going to take me fourteen months to complete. Then my plan was to continue with their master's program in clinical social work.

I had studied for hours to prepare for my first exam in that last sociology class, so I took the test with confidence. When I received the test back, I had a 66%. I was so mad, and I began to have a conversation in my own head that went something like this: "What am I even doing in sociology? I hate these classes. How am I ever going to complete a bachelor's program in something I don't even like? God, what am I doing?"

All of a sudden, I heard a voice from behind me say, "Tara, you are going to Bible college." I physically turned around to see if there was someone there, but I knew this was God's voice. I asked Him if I could leave right then, and He said, "No, you need to finish this class." I sat there silent, not listening to the teacher, who had already begun lecturing. In my mind, I thought, *Lord, I'm going to need some confirmation on this.* I sat in class and texted my friend Bea. I told her I was unsure of what I was doing in school and that I was not really interested in sociology. I never mentioned in the text what God had spoken to me. I knew Bea was at work and she'd get the message later. I just sat there in class reflecting on what God had said to me.

Later that same day, Aspen and I were running errands. I was driving when my phone rang. I had forgotten my headphones and couldn't answer the phone, so Aspen answered it for me. I could hear Bea telling Aspen, "I need to talk to your mom."

Aspen said, "She is driving. She'll call you back."

I heard Bea say, "Make sure she calls me back. This is important."

When we got home, I called Bea back. She said, "I was so tired when I got home from work that I had forgotten to read your text. I went to get out of my car, and I heard the Lord say, 'Read Tara's text.' So I sat there and read your text message. Then, all of a sudden, I had a vision of you; you were in Bible college."

I was dead silent on the phone. I couldn't believe what she had just said. There was the confirmation that I had just asked the Lord for earlier that day. I told her everything that had happened in class, and we both were blown away by God's goodness. It took me only seven days to decline my California State University of Sacramento acceptance and apply and be accepted to William Jessup University in Rocklin, CA. I started my bachelor's degree in Christian leadership in the fall of 2017.

CHAPTER 8

Change My Heart and Change Me

Once again, I sat and thought of a way that I could change my living situation. I was reminded of my friend Toni's advice about changing myself. I still believe to this day that the advice I received from Toni was the best advice I have ever received. Come to think of it, this was the second time she had spoken truth into my life and challenged me. Her words were like an arrow that shot deep into my heart. I thought to myself, *I need my heart to change because I cannot and do not want to live with this anger anymore.* Suddenly it didn't matter that my parents weren't changing. My mindset changed, and I again thought, *Maybe I'm the one who needs to change.*

I began to ask God to change my heart and to create a clean heart in me. I went back to Psalm 51:10 and asked Him, "Create a clean heart in me, O God, and renew a right spirit within me." I wish I could say that this happened overnight, but I can't. This process was slow and steady, but God gave me tiny glimpses of hope that I could hold on to while my heart, mind, and will changed to glorify Him. On July 31, 2017, God revealed to me who was to be my future Kingdom spouse. God knows me so well. My true heart's desire is to marry a man who is in love with God more than anyone else. I know if a man loves God most of all, then he will surely know how to love me the way I need to be loved.

Even as I noticed changes in my own heart, I was still fighting the spirit of frustration because I wanted to see change in my parents. I really did not understand why they weren't changing. I complained to God about them and their choices. I told Him why I was mad, frustrated, and angry. Finally, one day in my quiet time, the Lord spoke to me and said," Tara, your parents are not your responsibility. They are mine! I promise you, when they stand before Me, you will not be there with them."

I replied, "Well, then, what am I supposed to do?"

That's when His still, soft, quiet voice said, "Love them."

I cried because I did not feel like I knew how to love my parents. I had spent so much time blaming them and being angry at them that I had lost the understanding of how to love them. Once I let go of my desires and gave them to Him, the complete frustration that had been in my heart for years toward my parents vanished. Don't get me wrong. There are still times of frustration, but God has shown me that He is where I need to run when frustration sets in. He is the one who changes the situation, and He is the one who has changed me.

Remember when I found out I was pregnant with Aspen? I was scared and did not expect this to happen. I cried out to God and said, "Lord, what do

I do?" He said, "If you have this baby, it will be the hardest thing you have ever done in your life."

I began to question God about my daughter, who has been the most amazing daughter I could ever ask for! I began to ask God what I was going to have to go through that was going to be so hard.

He replied, "How has it been living with your parents these past several years?"

My jaw dropped! I realized right then and there that those words God had spoken to me fourteen years prior had nothing to do with my daughter. I now understood that He knew what I would go through and the process I would have to walk out. All of a sudden, I began to dissect what He had spoken to me: It would be the hardest thing I had ever done in my life. All at once, I realized I was going to accomplish that which God had set out for me to do. This was one of the most profound moments I have ever had in my life, and it gave me the boost I needed to accomplish the Father's will for my life. From that moment forward, I began to make conscious efforts to learn how to love my parents and to do it with a good attitude.

I surrendered to God's will and plan for my life because I now understood that He really did know me and that my life was predestined and in His hands. This didn't happen in one night, and honestly, it will be a process I go through for the rest of my days here on this earth. I thank God every day for the revelation that He put in my heart. I have changed so much in my feelings toward my parents, and I truly hope with all my heart they know how much I love and appreciate them.

One of the hardest places that I had to come to in my life was recognizing that I could not do this life on my own. I tried for about fifteen years to get to where I thought I would be happy, but nothing seemed to work. When I say I tried, I mean I tried everything—marriage two times, drugs, alcohol, partying, promiscuity…nothing worked. I felt like I had opened every door possible, looked inside, and said, "Nope, this isn't it," but I didn't see another way. I just felt like I was going to have to maintain until something fell from the sky and made my life different.

I prayed and asked God to help me. He again said, "If you continue in this lifestyle, you will not see Aspen graduate from high school." I blew off that word and thought, *Yeah, I will get to that sometime soon.* Four months went by, and I was sitting on the couch at home looking into the kitchen at Aspen during Thanksgiving of 2018. Again, that soft, quiet voice whispered in my ear, "Don't you want to see your daughter graduate from high school or walk down the aisle?" I got up from the couch and went in my room, where I ugly cried. I cried out to God and said, "I cannot do this. I need you! What do I do?"

I knew this was not possible through my own strength, so I decided to fast for three days and only drink water. The first day and night I literally just sat on my bed. I read the Bible every time I felt things getting crazy in my mind, so I basically spent ninety-eight percent of that first day reading the Bible. The second day I spent the same way because I knew if I left the house, I could not trust myself.

God, Change Me

On the evening of night three, when I laid down to go to bed, my heart was pounding so hard and so fast that I could physically see it. My nightshirt was rising and falling to the beat of my heart. I used my dad's blood pressure machine to test my pulse, and the results showed that my resting pulse was 93. I freaked out and called my friend who is an RN. She started asking all kinds of questions, and when I told her that I was fasting, she immediately told me my blood sugar was low and I needed juice or something sugary. I didn't want to break my fast until at least after midnight, but she explained that I needed to put something in my system. I had no juice and no sugar in the house. I just happened to look at the fruit plate, and there sat one single orange. She convinced me to just drink the juice, and immediately I could feel my heart rate drop and knew I was going to be okay.

I believe that it was within these three days that I fully surrendered my heart to Jesus and His plan for my life. I had no idea what that plan was, but I knew deep in my heart that I had really screwed up my life. I was willing to die at that point. I wanted to change so much that even if I died, I didn't want to go back to my old way of living my life. Drugs and alcohol were not the answer for me anymore. I was ready to trust God with everything.

During those three days, I grew to understand that I had to physically choose to make better choices. God told me He had a plan for my life, but I had to choose to walk it out; He was not going to do it for me. I was so used to the people in my life doing everything for me that this concept was a little frightening.

CHAPTER 9

What Is This New Heart You've Given Me?

WHEN I WOKE UP after the third night, there was something different about my mind. I felt peace for the first time in my life. I didn't have the same thoughts or those old desires. God literally plucked me out of the net of addiction. Psalm 25:15 says, "Mine eyes are ever toward the Lord; for he shall pluck my feet out of the net." I have not struggled with addiction in my life since then. He was faithful to deliver me from my own crappy choices, and I believe He always will as long as I am obedient to Him. I felt like I had a new heart, not a physical one but a spiritual one. I knew that God had changed it! For the first time in my life, I knew I could rely on Him to do what I could never do on my own.

I lived my life for over thirty years knowing that what I was doing was not right, but I was not willing to face my feelings. The Lord was faithful to help me understand I never have to do anything alone. He didn't create me to walk out this life alone. He will never leave me or forsake me. Not only that but His Word tells me and has proven to me that all I have to do is hold my peace, and He will fight for me (Exodus 14:14).

I will always continue to be amazed. It was as though I were physically drowning while I struggled through this process of surrendering my life to Jesus. It was truly the hardest part of my journey. However, the second I surrendered, He showed up to make it all worthwhile. I now understand that God created us in a way that makes us have to choose Him. He is truly a gentleman; He doesn't just come along, grab your hand, and say, "You're coming with Me." No, He allows us to grow and struggle until we come to Him. That process was so beautiful—painful but beautiful.

It was like I could see the door I had to walk through, but the doorway was lined with shards of glass. I was so ready that I truly didn't care if walking through the door actually killed me! As I approached the doorway, I was overcome with an amazing sense of peace. Just as I touched and walked through what I thought would cut me, every shard of glass turned into a beautiful feather that brought amazing relief. Those feathers were the wings of the Father that He talks about in Psalm 91:4. They covered me, and all of a sudden, I was truly safe!

That surrender brought all kinds of feelings I had never experienced. I was sad and angry with myself because I realized how I had wasted a lot of my life being rebellious! Every time I tried to condemn myself, however, the Lord was faithful to whisper in my ear, "Tara, you are forgiven, and I love you." He knew exactly what I needed each step of the way. This process was not a one-day thing. It has taken decades, and I believe it will take my lifetime to grow into the person God created me to be. In those years, I learned who God really is.I realized that I had been raised to rely on people and not on the one who created all people. I had allowed my heart to become hard, angry, and bitter toward my family. I blamed my parents for not protecting me and teaching me, and truthfully, I hated them. I knew my whole life that there was more to this life than what I was living. I just didn't know how to get to the answers or, to be honest, what I was even looking for.

I have spent most of my life trying to figure out love instead of allowing love to infiltrate my heart. Letting go and giving up the control of my heart and life were the hardest things I have ever done. I thought for a long time that I had given my heart to Jesus, but I had not. I thought I was thinking for myself, when in fact I was allowing the devil to control my life and the decisions I was making. This was because I didn't have a clear picture of who I was.

My heart was more wounded than I even realized. My thoughts about who God is were so skewed because of my perception. I was raised to rely on a person, namely, my mother, not on God. Therefore, when that person failed me, as all people do at some point, I was shaken and didn't know how to respond. I did what I knew would take the pain away, and that was drugs and alcohol.

Jesus helped me realize I had made choices that had affected my entire life. Some of those choices were because of life circumstances, and some were reactions to what was done to me. However, I had control over my choices, and I could change the direction that my life was going if I would trust Him fully. Jesus had never been so real to me as He was in those moments when I set time aside for Him. Jesus is real, and He showed up to prove that to me. My life is forever changed.

CHAPTER 10

God, Renew Your Righteous Spirit Within Me

IN THE SPRING OF 2019, I met with a therapist, Sarah, who had created a program called Bridges. She had studied the brain and understood how the right and left hemispheres of the brain communicated in both healthy and unhealthy people. I wanted to be a volunteer in this program she had created, which was at my local church. Before I could volunteer, however, I needed to be trained in the program. Sarah was leaving California to move across the country, and she was leaving her program with her friend Lisa, who was going to head up the program at our church.

This training usually takes about six to eight weeks, depending on the group size and the questions people have. Sarah offered to do the training one on one with me, meeting one or two times per week. I was so excited because this was one of the types of therapy I wanted to be involved in—art therapy. Bridges uses different mediums of art to bring out different issues and traumas that the brain sometimes files away. There is a lesson, then a project that is in line with the lesson, and then an art medium that is used to build the bridge that has been damaged between the left and right hemispheres of the brain from past traumas. This process can create incredible healing in a person who has suffered trauma in their life. It works for physically, emotionally, sexually, and even verbally abused victims.

As I was going through this training, we came to a week where she was talking about the effects of the different types of abuse, like sexual, physical, mental, and emotional abuse, as well as the different symptoms a person might have struggled with in their life. As I was reading through the list of symptoms, I started to feel lightheaded, overwhelmed, and a little dizzy. There were way too many of these symptoms that I could personally relate to, and I started to feel this heat come over me.

I asked Sarah, "What are the chances that a person could have suffered from ninety percent of these symptoms, but nothing has happened to them?"

She replied, "I cannot tell you how many people I train who go through this same realization." Then she said, "It doesn't happen. Our brains have a way of filing things away to protect us from the trauma."

I felt like my life started playing really quickly through my mind. Sarah asked me if I was okay, I told her I was, and we finished the lesson.

When I went out to my car, I just sat there and reread over the symptoms. I was blown away at how many of them I had lived in my life. The only area that I didn't feel like I had similarities was the verbal abuse areas. In reality, my second husband used to scream, curse, and yell at me all the time. I thought to myself, *I definitely know I have had that type of abuse in my life, but since I was an adult, would it affect me the same way?*

Over the next several days, I prayed and asked God to show me what had happened to me. I felt so vulnerable yet completely relieved. For the first time in my life, I finally understood why I acted the way I did as a young child. The fact that I exhibited perverted sexual tendencies and did strange things with my friends when I was young began to make sense. I was starting to put together the pieces as to why I had night terrors and nightmares a lot as a child. I realized now that I was a victim of sexual abuse and a perpetrator of this type of abuse also. There was abuse going on as far back as I could remember, and it was always brushed off like it was "just kids exploring."

I spent the next several days praying, crying out to God, and confiding in a trusted friend, Shannon, who was more like a mentor. She prayed with me, and because she's prophetic and has a God-led influence, she helped me realize that what I was beginning to understand was in fact true and that God would show me in His timing. At that point, I remember praying to God and telling Him, "I do not care what happened to me—I choose to forgive. I do not need to know—I choose to forgive. After all, this person was abused too, and this is why he did this to me."

At this time, I still don't remember exactly what happened, but I can remember up to a certain point; then the memory is just blank. I remember walking down a hall into a bedroom when I was five or six years old. I remember the color of the paint on the walls and the color of the bedspread. I would ask, "What are you doing?" and he would reply, "Come up here. I want to show you something." I would climb onto the bed, and the memory just becomes blank.

I began to recognize when I started to have extreme rage and anger problems. I even remember doing drugs at the age of nine just to get the anger to stop. I felt like being high was being in control because the anger was not there. As a child, I began to explore sexual things that were not normal, but I didn't understand where or why this was happening. I suddenly I realized I was okay. I wasn't the "evil spawn of Satan." I was abused, and it helped to understand this. This realization helped me to forgive myself fully, and at this point, I felt I never needed to know what happened.

In the middle of February 2020, I was driving home from the barn after spending time with my daughter's horse, Beau. I began to think and ask God if there was ever a time in my life when I was pure because I couldn't remember a time when I said no to sexual things. In an instant, He reminded me of a time when I was in a garden shed with a boy; I was about thirteen. I really liked this boy, and I thought he was cool because he was older than me. I was looking around at some stuff in the shed when he called my name. I turned around, and there he was with his pants down and his penis erect and hanging out. When he asked me to touch it, I ran out of there as fast as I could and didn't stop until I got all the way home! I was freaked out, to say the least, but this was exactly what I had asked the Lord about, and He reminded me.

As I continued driving home, I turned up the

radio, and Tauren Wells's song, "Fully Known," was playing. I sensed the Holy Spirit, and then I heard His voice say, "Tara, you will have to know." I knew exactly what He was talking about. I began to weep and cry out to my ABBA Father.

I said, "I trust you, Lord. Let it be as You have said."

He then said, "I need you fully healed, and you will have to know so that you can go through the process and be restored for what I have in your future." I cried all the way home, and as I write this chapter, I am still trusting in and waiting on His perfect timing.

CHAPTER 11

Thank You, God, for Changing Me

I AM COMPLETELY AMAZED at how God has changed my heart toward all of my family. I have a love for them like I have never felt before. My identity is found solely in the one who has created me, and this has helped me to fully forgive and move forward. I have never in my life been more excited for my future than I am right now. I am certain that God will restore me to the person He created me to be. I spent my whole life trying to fix myself, and all I had to do was surrender to the one who created me.

God showed me that my behaviors and attitudes

needed to be adjusted to accept change from the only one who could truly change me. I truthfully believe that the only way a person can gain lasting change is by fully surrendering to the Holy Spirit. I had to allow the Holy Spirit to empower me to make the lasting changes that I was seeking to make. I have experienced this in my own life, and I know this to be true. I spent the better part of thirty years trying to change myself and my life. Nothing that I ever tried had lasting value.

I believe we are all uniquely created to change this world. We are the change agents that God has created to bring the Kingdom of Heaven to this earth— "in earth as it is in heaven" (Matt. 6:10). If a person is truly born again through the Spirit of God, then the seed they carry comes alive with that first drink of water—accepting Jesus as their Savior. When this seed is watered continually through reading God's Word, it can bring a harvest that produces characteristics (the fruit of the Spirit, Galatians 5:22–23) that can change a person's world and, in effect, change the whole world.

The seed that God created us with inside our very being needs water to produce a harvest. Jesus was known throughout the world as the Great Thirst Quencher. John 7:37–39 says (paraphrased) that Jesus cried out after the last day of the feast, "If anyone thirsts, let him come to me and drink." John 4:14 says, "But whosoever drinketh of the water that I shall give him shall never be thirsty; but the water that I shall give him shall be in him a well of water springing up into everlasting life." The seed inside of us needs water to grow. This growth produces fruit that creates lasting change, not just in our hearts but outwardly in our lives. We change, and the fruit is visible. This produces the power to change old behaviors into new behaviors, and those new behaviors have the ability to change the world.

As I came to this realization, I began to understand that I needed to relinquish control of everything to the authority of God. This meant I had to start reading the real instruction book of life, the Bible. I decided that no matter what my physical body was doing, I was going to spend time in the Word each day until it changed my physical actions. You know what? It worked! I began to feel this love I had never experienced before. I began to look forward to reading the Bible every day, and I could feel it changing me from the inside out. My heart was beginning to grow and was feeling things it had never felt before. It was starting to recognize the unconditional love of the one who created me.

I don't know if I was like anyone else when it came to this process, but boy, was this a process. Nothing happened overnight for me—it usually doesn't happen that way—but God began to take me on this beautiful journey. The first thing I remember happening was my strong desire to know and understand Him and His plan for my life. I had this strong sense that there was so much more to life than what I was experiencing. I didn't expect life to be perfect, but something inside of me began to believe the words I was reading each day as I spent time in His Word.

In the Bible, there is an amazing story recorded in the book of Exodus in chapters 15 through 22. There was a group of people called the Israelites, and God allowed them to wander in the wilderness for forty years. In the wilderness, God provided everything they needed, such as food, clothing, and shelter. They took forty years to make a trip that should have taken them less than two weeks. The Israelites grew weary when God didn't act in their timeline and rebelled. They made idols. They complained. They turned their backs on God several times.

Similarly, for me, the wilderness is a place where I got complacent, and it became a place of comfort for me. The devil uses our weaknesses against us to get us to stay in our wilderness, just like the Israelites wandering through the desert for forty years. I think we can do this metaphorically if we are not careful. The Bible says the devil is a disguiser himself; he comes as an angel of light. Peter warns us in 1 Peter 5:8, "Be sober, be vigilant; because your adversary the devil, as a roaring lion, walketh about, seeking whom he may devour." The devil can and will destroy you if you give him the opportunity. You must participate in this fight against the devil. Use the Word of God against the devil, and send him back to hell, where he was sent by Jesus (Revelation 20:10).

CHAPTER 12

Thank You, God

I CHOSE FOR YEARS to never allow myself to process any pain, but I have processed a lifetime of pain in the last ten years. I now choose to forgive in all circumstances because forgiveness has given me freedom. We all make choices and decisions every day. Even when we do nothing, we are still making a choice to not do something that could have changed the course of our history.

I am getting used to this new heart, although it doesn't function in ways that I am familiar with. Sometimes I have to press through the vulnerability and embrace it as my "new normal." It's uncomfortable at first, but I've learned to just relax and enjoy this ride called life. My "new normal" is exciting and sometimes frightening—not frightening in a bad, scary way but an exhilarating and exciting scary that I know will have a happy ending.

There has been a lot of chaos in the world lately. It is my truest desire to make sure that anyone who reads this book has the opportunity to come into a relationship with the Father, if you desire (see Appendix A). God wants a deeper relationship with us all, if only we would take the time to draw close to Him. I hope that this book has helped you to not feel alone. I know that no one has walked in my shoes except me, but looking back, I remember how much easier it could have been to know that I was not alone and that I wasn't the only one to make such hugely foolish choices in my life.

Jeremiah 29:11 says, "For I know the thoughts that I think toward you, saith the Lord, thoughts of peace, and not of evil, to give you an expected end." I realized that in my whole life, I had yet to experience real hope or purpose. I had always chosen everything

I had done in my life because I thought the important things were to work, make money, and survive. This scripture was telling me something very different.

Psalm 51:10 says, "Create in me a clean heart, O God; and renew a right spirit within me." This verse cuts deep into my heart. I had not understood that God's Word was actually declarations that I could speak over myself, but I believe in Jesus, so His words have the power to change me. Immediately I began declaring these and a plethora of other scriptures over my life. These words began to change how I saw myself and began to change me from the inside out. I started to see God in a new way, as fully committed to me and how He created me. These beautiful words completely changed my heart and have continued to change me into the person He created me to be. I am by no means a perfect person. Only Jesus can ever fill those shoes. However, I am most certainly a changed vessel, and it is one hundred percent because of the choices I made to take God at His Word, believe what He says about me, and live that way. I had to choose to be an active participant in this process.

Thank You, God

No words can even come close to the gratitude I feel when I think of my Savior Jesus, my Papa God, and the Holy Spirit. I cannot even begin to remember how many times I have let them down. I have grieved the Holy Spirit and asked for forgiveness more times than I care to remember. However, there has never been a time when He has ever turned His back on me. I can guarantee that I have given Him multiple reasons to turn away from me, but He never has and never will.

It's amazing to me, looking back on all these things, that God's hand was there guiding me through all this stuff that was so difficult. His peace was with me and surrounded me so often that I didn't even see it until after a lot of this was over. Surrendering my life and heart to Jesus was clearly the best choice I ever made in my life.

There have been some specific things that the Holy Spirit has brought to my mind as I sit and write these words to you. One of the most helpful things I ever heard was from a mentor who always says, "Your feelings have nothing to do with your faith!"

I remember the first time I heard her say this—I wrote it down. I stared at it for a minute and sensed the Holy Spirit say, "Yes, Tara, those are two separate things that have nothing to do with each other." This revelation that the Holy Spirit showed me helped me to understand just how much control I have over my own actions. Not only do I have power but I have the power to say no.

Another thing the Holy Spirit has taught me is perseverance, and I don't mean the type of perseverance you need to finish a class or run a race. I am talking about Him giving me a promise then walking with me through my healing until I get to that promise. This is the perseverance it takes to be patient (sometimes for years) and wait with joy and expectancy. This type of perseverance only comes from Him.

The Holy Spirit is the best person to hang out with on a Friday night…well, any night really. I am learning new things every day and gaining knowledge and wisdom in Him. The Holy Spirit is the part of God we get to carry with us everywhere we go. His

Word says He never leaves us. Once we accept Him as our Savior, His Holy Spirit comes to live inside of us. He never leaves us.

Once I realized who I am in Jesus, a lot of the questions were answered where purpose was concerned. My heart has come alive to different things. My desires have changed, my thoughts have changed, and my heart has changed.

The final thing that I have learned throughout this beautiful process of life so far is that I am only responsible for my own actions and how I respond to others. I do not have to partner with anyone else's feelings on any given matter. I will not be standing with anyone else when I see Jesus face to face. I am only responsible for me and my life, and I intend with everything that I can to humbly walk this amazing life out, hand in hand with the one who created me.

My heart is overwhelmed by the Father's love for me. I lived my entire childhood feeling like my life did not matter. The one thing I know for certain is that my life matters to HIM. This reality had to travel from my head to my heart, and that journey took me forty-plus years to complete. Now I can really live the life that I was intended to live.

Thank you, God!

APPENDIX A

THIS IS A SIMPLE prayer that you can pray if you truly want to have a relationship with Jesus.

> *Lord,*
>
> *Thank you for opening my eyes to recognizing I need you. I believe that Jesus came to the earth as a man, died for me, and rose from the dead. I am a sinner and am sorry for choosing my own way. Please forgive me. As an act of my will, I surrender my heart to you. Please come into my heart and change me. I welcome your Holy Spirit to lead me and live in my heart. I want to follow and trust you as my Lord and Savior. Amen*

God, Change Me

There is a huge party in heaven right now since you've prayed this prayer! Congratulations! You just stepped into the most exciting relationship you will ever have. If you do not have a Bible, I would suggest you get one. The easiest translation, in my opinion, is the New Living Translation (NLT).

Stay in the Word to stay strong!

CPSIA information can be obtained
at www.ICGtesting.com
Printed in the USA
FSHW011123050621
81984FS